COSTUME of ANCIENT ROME

DAVID J SYMONS

drawings by Jack Cassin-Scott

B T Batsford Limited   *London*

In memory of my father,
William John Symons

Typeset by Tek-Art Ltd, Kent
and printed in Great Britain by
Anchor Brendon Ltd
Tiptree, Essex
for the publishers
B T Batsford Limited
4 Fitzhardinge Street
London W1H 0AH

British Library Cataloguing in Publication Data

Symons, David J.
    Costume of Ancient Rome. — (Costume reference).
    1. Costume, Roman — History
    I. Title   II. Series
    391'.00937   GT555

ISBN 0 7134 5327 3

Contents

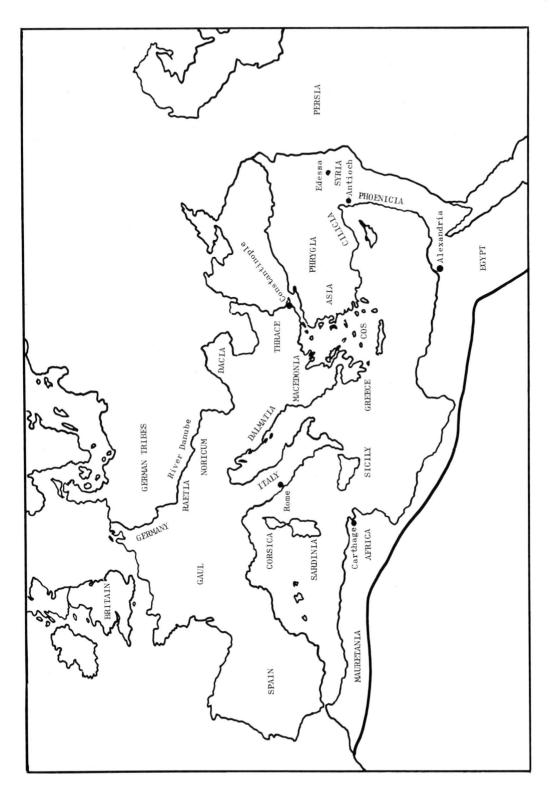

1   The Roman empire in the late
second century AD

1   Setting the scene

Our knowledge of the costume of the Roman world is derived from a number of sources. We have a series of contemporary written references that range from the asides of poets, historians and satirists to the rare but valuable inscriptions that bear upon the subject. Next there is the vast amount of pictorial evidence in the shape of mosaics, wall-paintings, large and small scale sculptures in stone, clay and metal and even the designs on coins. Finally there are the results of archaeological excavations which, while they have presented us with only a small number of preserved textiles, have allowed us to fill out our understanding of the technology used, for example, in weaving.

It should be pointed out, however, that major problems can arise in using these sources. It is frequently difficult, if not impossible, to be sure that we have always matched up the literary and the pictorial evidence correctly, while for some types of clothing (like underclothing) we have almost no evidence beyond the literary. We should also realize that our evidence is heavily biased in favour of the better off and also of the urban population as these were the groups that tended to be represented in art. For this reason depictions of country folk and of the urban poor are rarer.

A word of definition is also required. The Roman Empire at its height stretched from Scotland to the Sudan and from Spain to Syria (figure 1). Although this book deals with 'Roman' costume a vast number of people within the empire, while technically Roman citizens, belonged to very different cultural traditions and this was inevitably reflected in the way they dressed. Thus the 'Roman' in the title of this book should be taken to refer to the costume of the inhabitants of Italy and of the strongly Romanized areas of the empire and also of those people in all the provinces who adopted Roman ways. In chapter seven we will look briefly at the costume of Roman Britain to see how this situation was reflected there.

Materials

The textiles available to the Romans consisted mainly of woollens and linens but also included cottons and silks. Wool and linen were produced within the empire, as was a form of silk made on the Greek island of Cos using the cocoons of wild silk moths. Cultivated silk, however, until its introduction in the sixth century AD, had to be imported from China while cotton came from India. We also know of a cloth known as *cilicium* which was made from animal (generally goat) hair and was used to produce coarse, hard-wearing clothes. These were particularly favoured by fishermen and sailors for their resistance to damage by sea water.

In addition to textiles, leather and furs were also used to a lesser degree to make clothing. The *Edict on Prices* issued in AD 301 by the emperor Diocletian lists the maximum prices to be charged for a variety of animal skins, including sheep, beaver, bear, fox and leopard.

Technology

The spinning-wheel was unknown to the Romans so all yarns were spun using a distaff and spindle (figure 2). No specimens of the wooden looms used have survived but from the literary and artistic evidence it is clear that varieties of the upright loom were normal. A form of horizontal loom appears to have been used for the specialist weaving of silks and other fine textiles in the production centres of the eastern Mediterranean region. In addition tablet weaving was known and was used for the production of bands and braids.

Using this technology the Romans were able to produce a wide variety of textiles ranging from plain weaves to extremely complex twills, including the checkered cloth (*scutulata*) for which the northern provinces were known. In the case of silk, an extremely expensive luxury item, cloth was sometimes produced which mixed silk and woollen or linen thread.

The art of felt-making was also known and felt was used to produce hats and other garments. Knitting needles have been found on archaeological sites but knitting does not appear to have been common. Finally hairnets were made using a warp-plaiting technique known as sprang.

Colour

Woollens and linens might be left their natural colour – in the case of wool a range of shades from white and off-white through yellow-browns and red-browns to grey – or they might be bleached using sulphur. Men's tunics were commonly a shade of white as indeed were some women's but women seem generally to have preferred coloured clothing.

Dyeing was generally carried out on the spun yarn rather than on completed cloth. Among the Romans it was a large-scale process carried out by professional dyers. A range of colours could be produced using vegetable, animal and mineral dyes.

Yellow could be produced using saffron and reseda (an herbaceous plant). Nut-gall produced black and woad blue. Madder and archil (obtained from lichen) gave various shades of red while the shellfish *Murex brandaris* produced purple. In addition greens and browns were also known. Alum seems to have been the mordant normally used to fix the colours, whose shades could be varied by manipulating the amount of alum, the strength of the dyeing solution and the dyeing time.

Supply

Certain areas were famous for particular kinds of fabrics. High quality woollens were produced in Gaul, Germany, Phrygia, Noricum and Raetia and linens in Cilicia, Syria, Phoenicia and the city of Alexandria in Egypt. Silk was particularly associated with Phoenicia. Conversely we know that Africa and the city of Antioch in Syria produced very cheap clothing.

The less expensive linens and woollens worn by the bulk of the population were generally produced locally. Weaving and dyeing seem to have been specialist occupations and it appears to have been normal for even the poorer members of society to buy their clothes ready made. Surviving tunics from the later years of the empire frequently show tucks sewn into the fabric to adjust them to the wearer. In contrast the huge estates of wealthy landowners seem regularly to have included slave craftsmen who produced clothing for the workers on all their owner's properties. Furthermore from the third century AD onwards the state ran its own linen and woollen mills and dye works to supply clothing for the army and the civil service.

2 A woman spinning yarn using a distaff and spindle

Chronological Table

(Including persons named in the text. Names of emperors in capitals)

753 BC	Traditional date for the foundation of Rome.
509 BC	Traditional date for the establishment of the republic.
509-275 BC	Roman conquest of Italy.
264-202 BC	First and Second Punic Wars with Carthage. Sicily, Sardinia, Corsica and part of Spain become Roman provinces.
214-146 BC	Wars with the Macedonian and Syrian kingdoms. Third Punic War with Carthage. Macedonia, Greece and Africa annexed.
c **200-***c* **115** BC	Polybius, Greek soldier, politician and historian.
133-120 BC	Romans annex Asia and southern Gaul.
88-83 BC	Civil war between Marius (*c* 157-86 BC) and Sulla.
59-49 BC	Caesar (100-44 BC) conquers Gaul and lands in Britain.
49-45 BC	Civil war between Caesar and Pompey.
44 BC	Assassination of Caesar; renewed civil war. Control of the republic passes to Octavian, Caesar's great-nephew, and Marc Antony.
31-30 BC	Civil war between Octavian and Antony. Octavian wins and conquers Egypt.
27 BC	Octavian given the title AUGUSTUS and becomes the first emperor.
27 BC–AD **14**	Roman frontier advanced to the River Danube. Ovid (43 BC–AD 17), poet.
AD **14**	Death of AUGUSTUS.
41-54	CLAUDIUS. Annexation of Britain, Mauretania and Thrace.

78-84	Agricola (40-93) governor of Britain. Pliny the Elder (23/24-79), historian and encyclopaedist. Quintilian (*c* 35/40–*c* 100?), orator and lawyer.
98-117	TRAJAN.
101-106	Conquest of Dacia. Juvenal (*c* 50/60–*c* 130), satirist; Tacitus (*c* 56–*c* 115), historian; Pliny the Younger (*c* 61–*c* 112), man of letters; Suetonius (*c* 69–*c* 140), historian.
117-138	HADRIAN.
122-127	Construction of Hadrian's Wall. Appian (*c* 80/95–*c* 160), historian; Arrian (*c* 90–*c* 175), historian.
211-217	CARACALLA.
235-284	More than twenty emperors follow one another in quick succession. Civil wars, frequent barbarian attacks and an economic crisis wrack the empire.
284-305	DIOCLETIAN. Restoration of the empire.
301	The *Edict on Prices* issued.
307-337	CONSTANTINE I.
330	Foundation of Constantinople.
395	Separation of the empire into eastern and western parts.
406-476	Collapse of the western empire. Britain, Gaul, Spain, Italy and Africa settled by barbarians. The eastern empire, based on Constantinople, survives.
527-565	JUSTINIAN. Reconquest of Africa, Italy and parts of Spain.

2 Early Italy

Before its conquest by the Romans Italy was divided between a number of peoples of varied ethnic backgrounds and levels of civilization (figure 3). In the extreme south of the peninsula and on the islands of Sicily, Sardinia and Corsica were settlements inhabited by Greeks and Carthaginians, who had been establishing themselves there from the eighth century BC. In the north-west and north-east lived the Ligurians and the Veneti respectively. The bulk of northern Italy was dominated by the Etruscans. The centre and south central part of the peninsula was home to a group of more-or-less closely related peoples including the Picenes, Umbrians, Sabines, Samnites, Oscans and Latins. It was from the latter that the Romans themselves sprang.

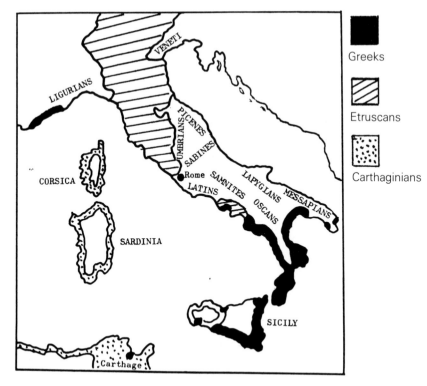

3   Italy in c 500 BC

Our information on the costume of these different peoples varies greatly. That of the Greeks and of the Carthaginians, who were descendants of emigrants from Phoenicia (the Lebanese-Syrian coast), is well-known and is covered in companion volumes of this series.* Of the Ligurians we know almost nothing.

The Veneti

The Veneti are known to us from the decoration embossed on their bronze *situlae* (bucket-like vessels) and other objects. These show the men wrapped in large, shapeless cloak-like garments that reach to the mid-calf. They also wear hats with more or less broad rims (figure 4). Women wear long tunics reaching to the calves or ankles and, over these, a long shawl or cape which fits tightly around the head and hangs low behind (figure 5). One crudely engraved female figure on a bronze plaque seems to wear a broad metal belt of a type known from slightly earlier excavated examples (figure 6).

Costume of Ancient Greece, David J Symons; *Costume of Old Testament Peoples*, Philip J Watson, Batsford 1987

4   Veneti: male costume, fifth century BC

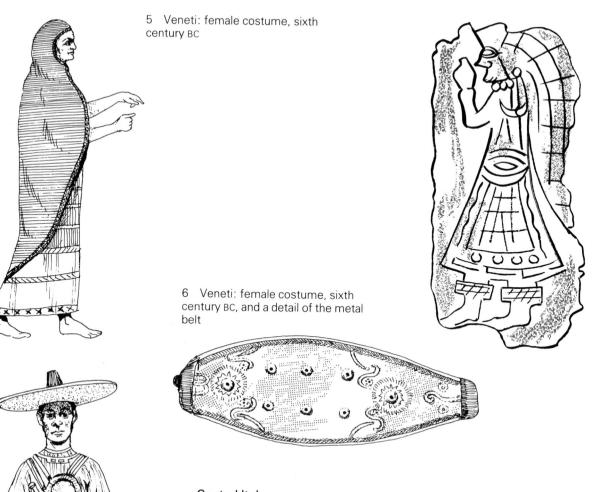

5 Veneti: female costume, sixth century BC

6 Veneti: female costume, sixth century BC, and a detail of the metal belt

Central Italy

The peoples of central Italy, the Picenes and Umbrians, may be represented by a more-than-life-size stone figure of a Picene warrior from Capestrano (figure 7). He wears a hat similar to those worn by the Veneti. Details of his clothing are difficult to distinguish but he seems to wear a tunic which is pulled up or cut-away at the sides and a small metal chest-protector, similar to excavated examples and to those we know were worn by the early Romans. In his right hand he holds a small axe.

7 Picene: the Warrior of Capestrano, sixth century BC, and a fourth century BC example of a chest-protector

11

Southern Italy

For some of the peoples who lived in the southern part of the peninsula we have a good deal of evidence for their appearance in the fourth century BC. By then they had been under Greek and Etruscan influence for many years and had seized control of a number of the Greek coastal cities. They then began to decorate their tombs with paintings mainly depicting scenes from funerals or from the funeral games that they held.

In these scenes women are shown dressed in flowing ankle-length tunics, girdled around the waist and with short sleeves. The tunics show what is either a tuck forming a flounce from above knee-level or a long fold of material hanging back down from the neck. When out of doors they wear cloaks or capes draped over their shoulders and pulled up over their heads (figure 8).

The men may be shown as warriors wearing armour and elaborate helmets over short tunics which, like that of the Warrior of Capestrano, seem to be either hitched up or scalloped at the hips (figure 9). When not dressed for war they wear short tunics and cloaks which may be wrapped closely around the body.

9   A Samnite warrior, fourth century BC

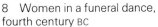

8   Women in a funeral dance, fourth century BC

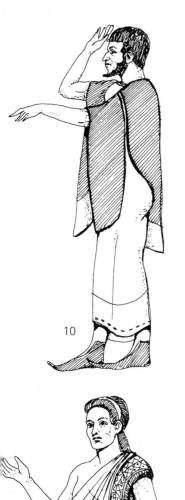

The Etruscans

It may seem paradoxical but the people about whose dress we are best informed are the traditionally mysterious Etruscans. Thanks to the discovery of large numbers of stone, metal and terracotta artefacts, and particularly to the vivid paintings in their tombs from the mid-sixth century BC onwards, we have an excellent picture of the way the (better off) Etruscans looked.

From the seventh century BC the Etruscans came under steadily stronger Greek influence and this is reflected in their costume.

Etruscan men wore a tunic which might either be cut very short or which might reach any length between the knees and the ankles. In addition to (or instead of) a tunic they wore a draped garment in a variety of forms. This was either simply hung over the shoulders, pinned at one shoulder or wrapped around the body (figure 10). One version of this draped garment, generally worn without a tunic beneath it, was known to Greek writers as a *tebenna*. This seems to have been the ultimate ancestor of the Roman *toga* (figure 11; colour plate 1).

Many of the tomb paintings show the Etruscans banqueting and dancing. In these the men were shown much more scantily dressed. Some revellers wore only a kind of skirt or kilt, which reached to the ankle and could be richly decorated (figure 12).

10

10   Etruscan man in a long tunic, wrap and pointed-toe boots

11   Etruscan man in a *tebenna* and boots

12   Etruscan man reclining at a banquet, dressed in decorated 'kilt'

12

11

Etruscan women generally wore an ankle-length tunic with short sleeves. The way the folds of these garments were represented makes it clear that some of these tunics were of a very fine material. It is also sometimes possible to see that a tunic has been fastened at intervals along the upper side of the arm and shoulder using small brooches, in a Greek style. The tunic was generally tightly girdled around the waist (figure 13), sometimes by a broad sash. Over this long tunic a second shorter one was sometimes worn together with, or instead of, a thick cloak like that worn by men. This was worn in the same styles as the male garment or could be pulled up over the head (figures 13 and 14; colour plate 1).

Both sexes were fond of brightly coloured clothes, magnificently decorated with embroidered or woven detail. In one case this extends to large human figures shown on a *tebenna* in a tomb painting. In another painting a woman's cloak clearly has a lining of a contrasting colour sewn in.

Women are also shown adorned with large amounts of elaborate gold and silver jewellery. This includes earrings, necklaces, bracelets, brooches, diadems and the like. Plentiful examples of this jewellery have been found and their discovery early in the last century was largely responsible for the nineteenth century vogue for 'Antique Revival' jewellery.

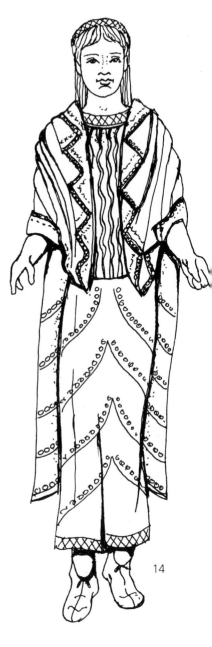

13 Two Etruscan women in long, girdled tunics, one with a cloak pulled up over her head. Both wear pointed-toe shoes

14 Etruscan woman in a long and a short tunic with a cloak draped over her shoulders

15 Etruscan man wearing a *tutulus*

The Etruscans commonly wore sandals or low shoes but they were particularly famous for a variety of footwear with long, pointed, curled toes (figures 10 and 13). These were often elaborately decorated suggesting that they may have been made of embroidered material as well as leather. Boots were either laced (figure 11) or pulled on. A particular form of boot sometimes shown had a plain toe and the top of the boot turned down.

A specifically Etruscan item of headgear was the *tutulus*, a kind of conical hat or cap which might again be richly decorated with embroidery. It was worn by both men and women (figure 15).

More normally worn only by men was a hat with a low crown and broad rim similar to those worn by the Veneti and the Picenes (figures 4 and 7). This seems to have been more in favour in the northern Po region than in Tuscany.

Down to around 500 BC Etruscan men were bearded and wore their hair long, falling over the shoulder (figure 12). From then on shaving appears to have been universal and the hair was also cut short. Female hair styles underwent a series of changes. In essence they went from long hair to cascading curls beside the face to braids bound around the head and finally back to curls, although obviously individual taste dictated the exact style worn.

In a number of scenes Etruscan men are shown in military costume and this shows very strong Greek influence. Warriors wore greaves and crested helmets and carried the Greek *hoplon*, a large round shield. Body armour consisted of padded linen or scale cuirasses. (See chapter 6 for a discussion of scale armour). These were worn over a short tunic. As offensive weapons they generally carried spears and swords (figure 16).

By the end of the third century BC all the peoples mentioned in this chapter had been conquered by the Romans. By the time of the empire their descendants had become completely Romanized, although the areas of southern Italy and Sicily settled by the Greeks continued to have a strongly Greek flavour throughout the period of the empire.

16 Etruscan warrior in scale armour and a short tunic. He wears greaves and a crested helmet

3 Male costume
of the Republic and Early Empire

Roman clothing for both men and women was divided into underclothes (*indutus*) and outer garments (*amictus*). People generally slept in their *indutus* and put on their *amictus* when they got up. Overnight the *amictus* could be used as extra bedding.

Underclothes

Underclothing for men consisted of the *subligaculum* (*licium, subligar, campestre* are also terms used). This was a linen or woollen loincloth or kilt which covered the loins and was knotted around the waist. In the early days of the republic it appears to have been the only garment worn under the *toga*. Later, under Greek or Etruscan influence, the tunic was adopted. It is not clear whether the tunic replaced the *subligaculum* or was additional to it. Presumably either happened depending on individual taste. Those involved in manual labour or other active pursuits sometimes wore only the *subligaculum*. It was also the usual wear for gladiators (figure 17). In warm weather it continued to be the only thing worn under the *toga*.

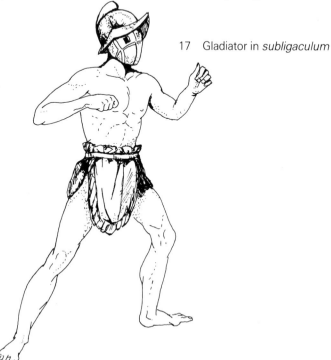

17   Gladiator in *subligaculum*

18   Roman citizen in a *toga* over two tunics. The projecting sleeve of the *subucula* can be seen clearly

16

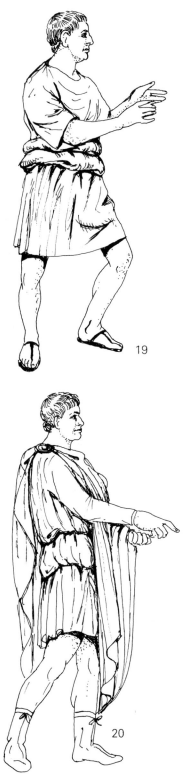

The under-tunic was known as the *subucula* or *tunica interior* and was initially made of wool, although linen became more common later. In cold weather a number of tunics could be worn beneath the outer clothing (figure 18). The historian Suetonius tells us that the emperor Augustus wore up to four tunics in winter beneath his *toga* although this seems to have been exceptional.

Tunics

Over these underclothes an outer tunic, the *tunica exterior*, would be worn. Indoors and on casual occasions this tunic was the normal wear of all classes of society. Outside of the upper classes a tunic and cloak seem to have been the normal outdoor clothing.

Tunics were made of linen or wool. The cut varied to individual taste but they might be sleeveless or have sleeves that varied from a few inches to wrist-length (figures 19 and 20). The evidence suggests that sleeveless tunics were made by sewing together two rectangles of cloth and leaving holes for the arms and head. Sleeved tunics, on the other hand, seem to have been woven as one cross-shaped piece of cloth with a slit left for the head. This cloth was then folded in half and sewn up down the sides and along the undersides of the sleeves.

Long sleeves were at first regarded as rather effeminate but became more common under the empire. The tunic width also varied according to taste, generally becoming fuller in later periods. Length was also variable but one writer, Quintilian, specifies that the tunic should reach just below the knees in front and slightly lower behind. Tunics were usually worn with a girdle or belt around the waist and the length was adjusted by pulling the fabric up through the belt, which was sometimes covered by the overhang of material (figure 20).

One variant of the tunic, the *tunica talaris*, reached to the ankles like female clothes but it was regarded as a distinctly effeminate form of dress. In general it seems that soldiers, slaves and workers tended to wear their tunics shorter and the aristocracy longer than the average.

19 Man in a tunic fastened with a broad, possibly woollen, girdle

20 Man in a tunic with long sleeves and a cloak. The two overhangs suggest that the tunic is belted twice. The cloak may be a *laena*

Working men are also shown wearing a version of the tunic known as the *exomis*. This was adapted so that it fastened over one shoulder only, generally the left, giving the other arm greater freedom of movement (figure 21).

Certain special forms of the tunic existed. Under the republic and early empire senators and knights (the *equites*, the financial middle-class) wore tunics distinguished by broad (senators) or narrow (knights) vertical purple bands. It is clear that the knight's tunic had single narrow bands falling from each shoulder, front and back. The nature of the senator's broad band has been fiercely debated but the evidence suggests that they were placed in exactly the same places as on a knight's tunic but were broader. The bands were either woven into the fabric or (less probably) were coloured strips darned to it (colour plate 4).

Another variant was the *tunica palmata*. This was an elaborately decorated garment, made of purple cloth with gold-thread decoration which originally depicted palm trees or palm branches. Under the republic it was worn by victorious generals but in imperial times it was restricted at first to the emperor and then to the emperor and the consuls.

The *toga*

The typical dress of the Roman male was the *toga*. As mentioned in chapter two this may be traced back to the Etruscan *tebenna*, a form of cloak worn wrapped around the body. It was originally worn by both men and women but seems to have gone out of fashion for women at quite an early date. However, as late as the early empire it might still be worn by adolescent girls and it was the legally prescribed wear for prostitutes. During the republic the *toga* grew steadily more bulky. The historian Pliny the Elder refers to a statue of the early fourth century BC which showed a man in a *toga* on horseback, an activity hard to imagine anyone trying while wearing the later *toga*. As the *toga* grew it became impossible to wear it for any sort of active pursuits and it was replaced by a variety of cloaks to be considered later.

Despite this the *toga* became the required wear for all formal occasions and was virtually the official dress of elected magistrates. It remained the regular form of dress for the upper classes into the early empire. By that time it was, according to our best evidence, a semi-circular woollen cloth about 5-5.5 metres long by 2-2.5 metres broad, although dandies were noted for wearing even larger *togae*. It seems that the *toga* was woven in one piece.

From statues showing the *toga* it is clear that the style of draping it varied with time and personal preference. However, a reasonably standard way (figure 22) was to let about one third of the length hang foward over the left shoulder, with the straight edge to the neck and the end hanging between

21   Man in an *exomis*

22   Man in a *toga* and holding a scroll

23 Man with his right arm enveloped in his *toga*

the feet. The rest of the *toga* was then brought around the back, under the right arm, across the chest and thrown back over the left shoulder so that the second end was left hanging down the back. The top edge of the part drawn across the chest was folded over and allowed to hang down in a large fold (the *sinus*) over the right thigh. In addition, that portion of the *toga* hanging from the left shoulder to between the feet (the first part put on) was grasped at the shoulder, pulled up and allowed to slightly overhang the *sinus* (colour plate 2). The *sinus* appears to have been a development of the end of the republic.

The *toga* might also be pulled up over the head for protection against the weather (colour plate 4). It was also possible, when putting it on, to bring it over the right shoulder, wrapping the right arm within it (figure 23).

The standard form of the *toga*, the *toga virilis* or *toga pura*, was made of wool left in its natural colour or slightly lightened. However, there were a number of varieties of the *toga* which were distinguished by their colour and decorative details and were worn by particular groups. The *toga praetexta* had a purple border along its straight edge and was worn by boys and youths up to the age of 14 to 16, when they assumed the *toga virilis*. It was also worn by those who had held the leading governmental positions (figure 24, colour plate 4).

The *toga candida* was artificially whitened with chalk and was worn by candidates standing for election as magistrates. The *toga pulla*, a black or dark coloured version, was worn as a sign of mourning. The *toga picta* was of purple cloth decorated with designs worked in gold and was worn with the *tunica palmata* by victorious republican generals. It later became the official *toga* worn by the emperor and the consuls. Finally the *trabea* had stripes of red and a purple border and was worn only by certain groups of priests.

As can be imagined the *toga* was an expensive and cumbersome piece of clothing. It was almost impossible to put it on single handed. Even with help it was difficult to drape it correctly and near impossible to keep it so during wear. For these reasons it gradually fell out of favour. Successive emperors in the first and second centuries AD issued decrees insisting on its use on certain occasions but early in the second century we find the Greek writer Appian commenting that in Italy slaves and free men were dressed the same except for those few occasions when the masters put on their *togae*.

At the same time Juvenal complains that, although the *toga* is never seen in the rest of Italy anymore, in Rome you are still obliged to wear it. Pliny the Younger counts not wearing the *toga* as one of the pleasures of leaving Rome for his country villa.

By the third century AD the *toga* was an anachronism worn only by extreme conservatives or on specific ceremonial occasions.

24 Little boy in a *toga*. Around his neck is a *bulla*

Cloaks

We know the names of a large variety of cloaks or capes which the Romans wore in inclement weather. Unfortunately it is often difficult to be sure what distinguished certain types from others, and even harder to identify them correctly in the surviving representations.

The *lacerna* was a light woollen cloak of rectangular shape which was worn over the *toga*. It had a fitted hood and was worn open and loose at the front, the only fastening being by a brooch at the shoulder. We hear of white, purple and dark coloured *lacernae*, as well as ones dyed bright colours.

Less fashionable (and less costly) than the *lacerna* was the *paenula* which was generally made of a thicker woollen cloth, although ones made of fur are also mentioned. The *paenula* was the normal bad weather wear of the less well-off and, like the other cloaks described below, was worn over the tunic (figure 25). It was also worn by all classes when travelling. It was tight fitting and totally or partially closed at the front (figure 85) so that it was put on over the head. It was frequently worn thrown back from the shoulder to leave an arm free. For added protection it might be fitted with a hood (*cucullus*). It seems to have normally been dark coloured although we hear of groups of slaves being fitted out with coloured *paenulae* as a kind of livery. The shape seems to have varied, being either round, rectangular or even bell-shaped. It was generally about knee-length.

25 Man in a tunic and *paenula*

Also hooded was the *birrus*, a rectangular cloak usually made of thick, coarse wool with a long, raised nap, although we also hear of *birri* made of beaver skins. Our sources describe the *birrus* as stiff compared to other more flowing cloaks (figure 26).

A type of cloak which dated back to republican times was the *laena* (figure 20). This was again made of wool, this time with the nap raised on both sides of the cloth, making it a thicker, warmer garment. It was worn by all classes of society, the wealthy favouring *laenae* of red and purple. Like the *lacerna* it was fastened by a brooch at the shoulder.

The woollen *abolla* also dated back to republican days and was fastened in the same way. It seems to have originally been a military cloak but, by the end of the republic, civilians had adopted it too. It was again worn by rich and poor alike in varying qualities of cloth. It is distinguished as a 'double' cloak which seems to mean that it was very long and was worn folded double. A coarsely made *abolla* was adopted as a kind of unofficial uniform by philosophers.

Another cloak of military origin was the *sagum*, a thick woollen cloak again fastened at the shoulder by a brooch. Like the *abolla* the *sagum* was also adopted by civilians. It appears to have been cut in a variety of styles and to have sometimes been fitted with a hood (figure 27). We are told that certain groups at Rome wore a red *sagum* while the Spanish preferred black and the Gauls check-patterned ones.

Roman officers, especially generals, wore the *paludamentum*, also

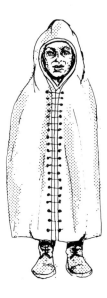

26 Man in a long *birrus*

known as the *sagulum* or 'little *sagum*'. Despite this name it was a larger, thicker, better quality cloak, often with a fringed border. Like the *sagum* it was pinned at the shoulder. Although we hear of white or dark coloured *paludamenta* the normal colour seems to have been purple and they could be decorated with designs worked in gold thread.

Some other cloaks should be mentioned. The *alicula* was a short cloak or cape reaching only to the elbows and regarded as suitable for boys or huntsmen. Two cloaks or wraps of Greek origin were also worn by some sectors of Roman society. The *chlamys* was a rectangular cloak of fine woollen material which was pinned with a brooch at either the throat or the shoulder (figure 28).

27   Man in a hooded cloak, probably a *sagum*

28   Man in a *chlamys*

The *pallium* was a Roman version of the Greek *himation*. It was a large, wrap-around garment, in some ways similar to the *toga* but smaller, lighter and square or rectangular in shape (figure 29). It was worn with one end hanging forward over the left shoulder and the remainder drawn around the back, under the right arm and then either flung back over the left shoulder or hung over the left arm. Wearing such Greek clothing tended to be frowned upon under the republic but its use became more acceptable with the empire.

The countryside

Rural labourers and the slaves who worked the large estates of the aristocracy sometimes wore a number of garments made of skins rather than of wool or linen. The *pellis manicata* was a long coat with sleeves while the *diphthera* is referred to by writers of the second century AD as a cloak made of skins. In addition there were sleeves (*manicae*) and leggings (*ocreae*) of hide which were also worn by huntsmen. Also worn for agricultural work, and by soldiers when doing dirty jobs, was the *cento*. The precise form of this is unclear but it was a patchwork garment of some kind, sewn together from pieces of old cloth.

Trousers

Trousers were worn by the Persians and other eastern peoples and by the Celts and Germans of the north. They were regarded by the Romans as rather barbarous and never became common articles of dress. They were, however, worn in certain circumstances, generally in the form of tightly fitting knee-breeches (*bracae* or *feminalia*). Their use seems to have been restricted to legionaries and others in the colder northern provinces (figure 30) and to protect the legs when riding a horse.

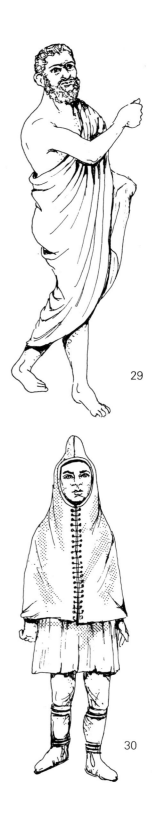

29

30

29   Man wearing a *pallium* without a tunic, in the Greek style

30   Man in a short *birrus* over a tunic and *bracae*

4 Female costume
of the Republic and Early Empire

31

32

In general the cut of female dress was very similar to that of male clothes. On the whole women's clothes were more colourful and, according to ancient authors, tended to be made from lighter weight, finer fabrics, especially silks and cottons. Needless to say only women belonging to upper class families could have afforded such expensive luxuries. For the bulk of the female population, as for the male, linens and more normally woollens would have been their usual wear.

Underclothes

Like her male relatives the Roman woman divided her clothing into underclothes and outer garments. A woman's underclothes basically consisted of the *tunica interior*, which might be cut with or without sleeves. Below this she might wear a loincloth (*subligaculum*) like that worn by men and possibly a *strophium* (also known as a *cestus*, *amictorium* or *mamillare*). This was a soft leather or linen band tied around the breasts. Since the *strophium* was intended to support or squeeze in a large bust it was not worn by every woman. It seems that the *strophium* could be worn over the *tunica interior* as well as below it. Those with a more matronly figure might wear a *capitium*. This seems to have been a stiff sort of garment rather like a corset and was worn over the tunic.

The *stola*

The standard item of outer clothing for a married woman was the *stola*, a long, full gown which was belted into overhanging folds below the breasts, and also sometimes at the waist. It reached down to partially cover the feet (figure 31). The *stola* could be decorated with a coloured band at the neck and with an *instita*, a broad flounce with many folds sewn around the hem. More common, and less expensive, than the *instita* was a border called a *limbus*, which was woven into the fabric of the *stola*. This might be a simple band in a contrasting colour or could be patterned (colour plate 4).

The stola might be made with (figure 32) or without sleeves (figure 31).

31 Woman in a sleeveless *stola*, girdled below the breasts and at the waist

32 Woman in a *stola* and a *palla* which is drawn up over her head

If it lacked sleeves the tunic below would often have them. Where sleeves occurred they generally reached to the elbow. The upper edge of the *stola* was sometimes not sewn but pinned by small brooches fastened at intervals along the arms and shoulders, fixing the back of the dress to the front (figures 32 and 33).

In place of the *stola* unmarried women wore a long *tunica exterior*, fastened by a belt and also reaching to the floor. This was often pinned along its upper edge in the same fashion as the *stola*.

The *palla*

In the early days of the republic women seem to have worn a *supparum* as an outdoor wrap. This was a long, shawl-like garment made of linen. Although we are not sure it was probably placed around the shoulders and hung down to the feet. By the late republic and early empire women generally wore a *palla* when out of doors.

The *palla* was a large, rectangular wrap of woollen cloth which could be draped according to individual taste and the dictates of fashion. A common method resembled the draping of the *toga*. One end of the *palla* hung forward from the left shoulder and the remainder was brought behind the back. It was then brought either under the right arm, around the right arm or over the right shoulder. The second end was then hung over the left forearm (figures 32 and 33). Alternatively the second end might be thrown back over the left shoulder (figures 34 to 36). The *palla* was often pulled up to cover the head as custom dictated that well-bred women should keep their heads covered when out of doors (figures 32 and 34). In some representations the *palla* is shown tied around the hips and knotted in front of the body (figures 37 and 38).

To complete her outfit a woman might wear a woollen scarf (*focale*) knotted at her neck. The *focale* was also worn by infirm or delicate men but its use was otherwise thought rather effeminate.

Other clothes

The *stola* with the *palla* was the normal female dress but we know of other garments which were also worn.

An alternative to the *palla* survived from early republican days. This was the *ricinium*, a smaller rectangular wrap. By the early empire it was worn only at funerals. After the funeral women would change into the *palla* for the mourning period. The *pallae* were black in the late republic but it seems that it became customary for them to be white under the empire.

The *crocota* was a light, gauzy robe which took its name from the saffron (*crocus*) with which it was dyed. It seems to have been something like a

33

34

33   Woman in a *stola* and *palla*

34   Woman wearing a *stola* and a drawn up *palla*

24

35 Little girl in a *tunica exterior* and *palla*

36 The draping of a *palla* seen from the rear

37 Woman in a *stola* with her *palla* tied around the hips

38 Woman wearing a *stola* and a *palla* tied around her

sleeveless tunic and in some cases was worn over a tunic. Another high quality robe was the *cyclas*. This was circular in shape and was distinguished by having a gold-inlaid border added to the bottom (figure 39). Although the *crocota* and the *cyclas* were both regarded as properly female wear they were also worn by foppish and effeminate men.

Finally, the *coa vestis* was made from the wild silk produced on the Greek island of Cos. It was a very fine, almost transparent gown favoured by women of easy virtue. It was sometimes dyed purple and woven with strips of gold (figure 40).

Cloaks

For wear during bad weather or while travelling the same range of cloaks and capes that has been described in the previous chapter would have been available to women. Judging as best we can from the evidence it would appear that the *paenula* was the most commonly worn.

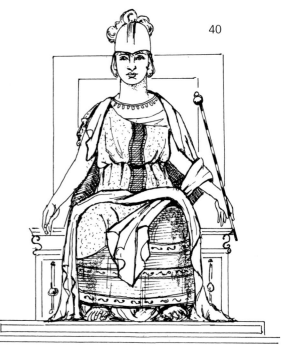

40

39

39 A personification of the goddess Roma. Her bordered lower garment may be a *cyclas*

40 A woman wearing what is probably a *coa vestis*, with a *palla* draped over her lap

The Roman bride

As is the case today tradition demanded that the Roman bride wore special clothing for her wedding day. Over her underclothes she put on a special tunic, the *tunica recta*, which was white and woven in one piece. This was fastened at the waist with a girdle (*incingulum*) made of wool and tied into a special double-knot, the *cingulum herculeum*, or 'knot of Hercules' (figure 41).

Her sandals were dyed saffron. Her hair was dressed in the prescribed fashion of six locks, parted with the point of a spear and tied with woollen ribbons (*vittae*). Over her head went a flame-coloured veil (the *flammeum*) which modestly covered the upper part of her face and fell around her to her feet. Over the veil she was then crowned with a wreath, originally made of verbena and sweet marjoram but later of myrtle and orange blossom. Dressed in this way she would be married in her father's house and then led in procession to the groom's house, where he had already gone to wait for her (colour plate 5).

The last garment to be considered is the famous Roman 'bikini'. This is known from a leather bikini bottom found in a London well dating to the second century AD and from a Sicilian mosaic of the early fourth century which shows girls wearing the complete ensemble (figure 42). The fact that the girls are doing gymnastics, which were not considered to be a suitable activity for respectable women, suggests that they were entertainers and that the bikinis were in fact stage clothes of some sort.

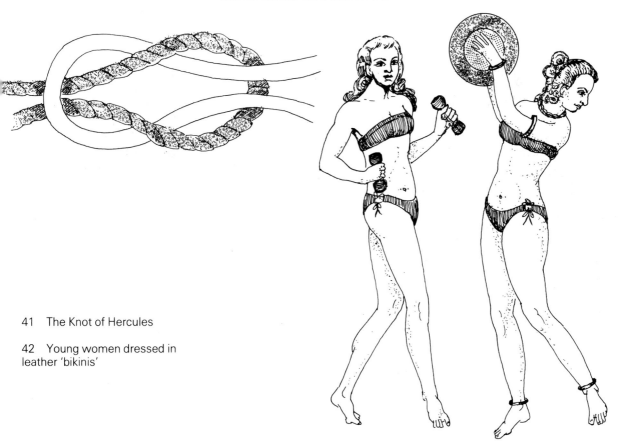

41   The Knot of Hercules

42   Young women dressed in leather 'bikinis'

5 Costume of the Later Empire

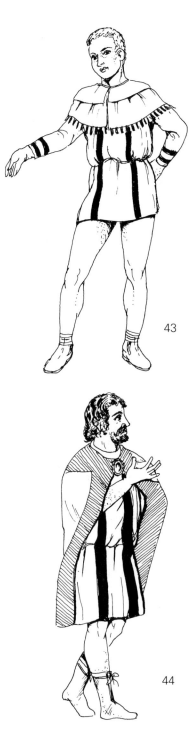

The period from the third to the sixth century AD saw the transition from the classical Roman to the Byzantine world. It is the period when Christianity became the state religion and the emperor changed from being the first citizen of the state to an autocratic ruler. Society became extremely regimented and an immense bureaucracy grew to oversee all aspects of life. However, people still spoke Latin and thought of themselves as Romans and the principal institutions of the early empire existed throughout the period.

While the basic varieties of clothing – tunics, wraps, cloaks – remained in use they tended to become fuller, longer and more richly decorated. The clothing of the imperial court and the aristocracy became more and more magnificent until, by the early sixth century, gold and jewels were regularly added to garments. Silk was more commonly used than before and, from the time of the emperor Justinian, was actually cultivated and produced within the empire. Linen seems to have been used more extensively by all levels of society in this period.

Underclothes

We have no real information about underclothes in the later empire and must assume that they were much the same as in the preceding period. In the fourth century we do hear of a linen tunic, the *camisia*, which seems to be the old *subucula* under a different name. One addition to the repertoire were the *hosa*, stockings which covered the legs and feet and which became normal in the fifth and sixth centuries (colour plate 7).

Tunics

Tunics tended to become longer and more roomy. Long sleeves (to the wrist) became more common (figure 43). Two new varieties of tunic came into fashion from the third century onwards, the *colobium* and the *dalmatica*. The *colobium* sometimes reached to the knee, like earlier tunics, and retained the same short sleeves but it was of a more generous cut (figure 44). Other versions might be as long as ankle-length. The *colobium* was worn by both sexes although women wore only the longer version (figure 45).

43 Man in a long-sleeved tunic and an *alicula*

44 Man in a *colobium* and cloak

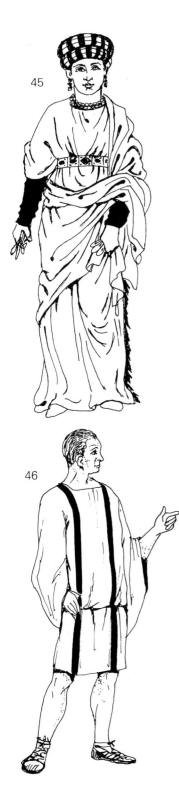

45

The *dalmatica* took its name from the province of Dalmatia where it originated. Its distinguishing feature was its long, loose sleeves (figure 46). From the emperor Diocletian's price edict we know that it was made in various qualities of wool, linen or silk. Like the *colobium* it was worn by both sexes. Men usually wore their *dalmaticae* calf-length (figure 47), women to the ankles or covering the feet (figure 48). From the fourth century women's *dalmaticae* tended to widen and to have the sleeves cut slanted rather than square.

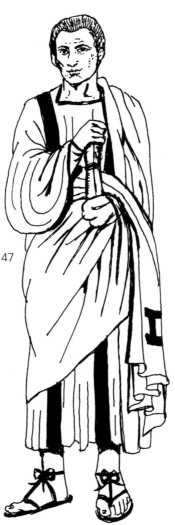

47

48   Woman wearing a *tunica talaris* and *dalmatica* below an elaborately draped *palla*. Around her shoulders she wears a jewelled *superhumeral*

46

45   Woman in a *tunica talaris*, long *colobium* and *palla*

46   Man in a *dalmatica*

47   Man wearing a *dalmatica* and *pallium* over a *tunica talaris*

29

Both the *colobium* and the *dalmatica* were frequently worn ungirdled (figures 49 and 50). When a girdle was worn it was generally placed at the waist or a little above it.

The *tunica talaris*, with long sleeves fitting tightly at the wrist, increased greatly in popularity from the third century as well. It was either worn on its own (figure 51) or beneath a *colobium* or *dalmatica*, showing only at the forearm or wrists (figures 45 and 48; colour plate 7). It was again worn by both sexes, at the same lengths as the *dalmatica*.

The adoption of these various tunics by women saw the gradual disappearance of the old *stola*. The *cyclas*, however, survived as a form of ceremonial dress into the fifth century.

50 Woman in a *dalmatica*

49 Man in a *dalmatica* and *pallium*

Tunic decoration

All these garments might be richly decorated. The *clavi* or bands which were discussed in chapter three came to be commonly used by all classes (figures 43 and 44). Diocletian's price edict gives prices for *dalmaticae* with or without purple stripes. *Clavi* did not, however, only take this form. Preserved specimens of tunics from Egypt that date between the fourth and ninth centuries have *clavi* made up of complicated patterns in red, yellow, purple, green and blue on the woollen or linen ground. On these tunics this decoration is worked in a tapestry technique where the weft of the fabric is replaced by the coloured wools.

In addition to *clavi* tunics usually had bands on the sleeves and frequently circular or square panels of decoration at the shoulders and above the knees (figure 52). These panels need not match each other and the same tunic might have completely different decoration in each. In the later part of our period the *clavi* often ran only from the shoulder to just above the waist and the decorative panels tended to disappear (figure 51).

52 Man in a decorated tunic

51 Man in a *tunica talaris*

It should be borne in mind that throughout this period the poorer elements of society would have been wearing shorter, less elaborate versions of these garments. In some representations working men are still shown wearing the off-the-shoulder *exomis* described in chapter three (figure 21).

Wraps

Over their tunics both men and women sometimes wore a wrap. Men now commonly wore the *pallium*, which had lost its earlier stigma. It was worn (figure 47) with one end hanging over the left shoulder in front of the body and reaching almost to the ankles. The remainder was brought around the back, under the right arm, across the front of the body and hung over the left arm. During the fourth century it began to be worn folded so that its width was much reduced (figure 49). Thereafter it was gradually reduced in size until it became effectively only a long, narrow band. In this form it survived as an ecclesiastical vestment.

Women continued to wear the *palla*, as described in chapter four (figure 45). From the fourth century the *palla* also became longer and thinner and was worn folded like the *pallium*. One end was allowed to hang in front of the body and was fastened by a girdle at the waist. The *palla* was then broadened out and passed over the left shoulder and across the back. It could then be brought under the right arm, allowed to drop to its full width and swept up over the left shoulder so that it hung down the back. Alternatively (figure 48), after being brought across the back, it might be passed over the right shoulder. It was then taken across the front of the body and under the left arm. It was now allowed to drop to its full width, brought around the back again, over the right thigh and up to the waist. It was then fixed in position with a girdle.

Cloaks

For outdoor wear the varieties of cloak described in chapter three initially continued in use. The *birrus* appears in Diocletian's price edict and we know from literary sources that *saga* made of Gallic and Spanish cloth were popular in Rome in the fourth and fifth centuries. The *alicula* appears frequently in sculpture and paintings (figure 43) as does the *paenula*, which under the new name of the *casula* was the ancestor of the clerical chasuble (figure 53). In some cases the *paenula* was decorated with *clavi* in the same way as a tunic.

Another outdoor garment, the *caracalla*, made its appearance at Rome early in the third century. According to tradition it was introduced by the emperor Marcus Aurelius Antoninus who received the nickname 'Caracalla' as a result. It had been in use in Gaul as early as the reign of Augustus, when it is described as a hooded, close-fitting cloak, with long sleeves and slits at front and back. The original *caracalla gallica* reached to the knees but the emperor lengthened it to the ankles and this longer version was named the *caracalla antoniniana* after him.

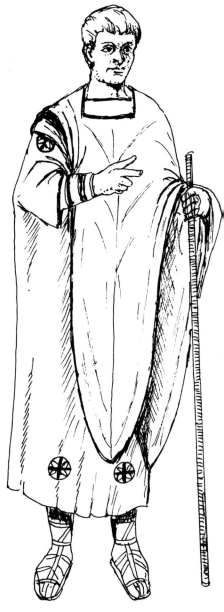

53   Man in a *casula*

PLATE 1 *Etruscan man and woman dancing*

PLATE 2 Slave helping his master put on his toga

PLATE 3 *An overseer and a group of slaves*

PLATE 4 *Roman senator and his family*

PLATE 5 *Bride being dressed for her wedding*

PLATE 6 *Officer addressing a group of soldiers*

PLATE 7 *Members of the imperial court in the sixth century AD*

PLATE 8 A rural scene in Roman Britain

During the latter part of the period under discussion, however, people normally wore a simple rectangular or semi-circular cloak of varying length. This was either pinned at the breast or shoulder, or it was draped over the shoulders and allowed to hang freely (figure 44). Women sometimes drew their cloaks up over their heads as with the *palla* (figure 54).

In the fifth century a long, semi-circular cloak known by the old name of *paludamentum*, but differing in shape from the earlier version, was adopted for male use at the imperial court. As such it finally superceded the *toga* which survived only as a ceremonial robe for consuls (see below). The empress was the only woman allowed to wear the *paludamentum* and she, like the emperor, wore one of purple – a colour restricted to their use alone. Similar cloaks were, however, worn by the ladies of the court. The *paludamentum* was distinguished by two rectangular embroidered panels (*tablia*), one to each side at the front (colour plate 7).

The empress and other women of the court also wore a broad, jewelled collar (the *superhumeral*; figure 48, colour plate 7). To complete their outfit women also commonly wore a headdress or veil (figures 48 and 50).

The *toga*

The *toga* has already been mentioned as an anachronistic survival at this period, initially as a court or ceremonial garment and later purely for the consuls. Like the *pallium* the *toga* steadily reduced in bulk, becoming longer and narrower and being worn folded so that the width was even further reduced. By the fifth century, when it was abandoned by all but the consuls, it was worn as follows (figure 55).

One end of the folded *toga* was hung forward from the left shoulder. The remainder, still folded, was drawn across the back to the right side of the waist, around the body and back up to the right arm. It was brought below this, across the chest, over the left shoulder and back again to the right side of the waist. At this point the folds were loosened and the end of the *toga* was drawn across the front of the body and allowed to hang over the left arm.

54   Woman wrapped in cloak

55   Emperor wearing an elaborately draped *toga* over a *tunica talaris*

Consular dress

The ceremonial clothing worn by the consuls in the later empire is illustrated on a series of ivory plaques distributed by the consuls to their friends as mementoes (figure 56). Over a long *tunica talaris* the consul wore a slightly shorter *colobium* which was richly decorated. Draped above this was his *toga picta*.

On the plaques one end of this *toga* hangs tightly folded in front of the body. The remainder passes over the right shoulder, back under the right arm, over the left shoulder and across the back, the folds being loosened on the way. It is then brought around the right side of the waist, across the front of the body and allowed to hang over the left arm.

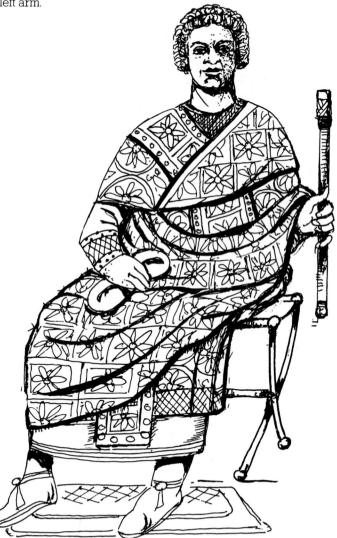

56 Rufius Gennadius Probus Orestes, consul for AD 530, in his consular robes

The charioteer

We will end this chapter by looking at the costume of a driver in the chariot races that aroused such enthusiasm among the later Romans (figure 57). Charioteers were dressed in short tunics in the colours of the team they represented – the Blues, the Greens, the Reds or the Whites. On their heads they wore low leather helmets. For further protection their chests were strapped up with leather bands or thongs and similar bands were tied around their upper thighs. Since they drove with the reins tied around their bodies, which meant that they might be dragged by their chariot teams if they crashed, each driver carried a curved knife (*falx*) in his belt with which he could try to cut himself free.

57   A charioteer in racing costume

6 Military costume

The soldier must have been a familiar figure at all periods of Rome's history and over a period of several hundred years his armour and weapons changed a great deal.

Under the early republic all citizens had to serve in the army if they were needed. As wars took place further from Rome and lasted longer the army came to consist of a professional force of volunteers. The emperor Augustus established a permanent standing army made up of legions of Roman citizens and of auxiliary units, recruited from allied and subject peoples. The legionaries were heavily armoured infantry, the auxiliaries supporting units of light infantry, missile troops and cavalry. Differences between the legions and the auxiliaries gradually lessened and, by the fourth century AD, the important distinction was between those troops guarding the frontiers and those forming mobile field armies based at key points within the empire.

The Republic

Our earliest detailed account of the Roman army was written by the Greek soldier and historian Polybius (c 200-118 BC). He describes four classes of troops. The youngest and the poorest men served as *velites*. These were light infantry armed with a sword and javelins. They wore no body armour over their tunics, relying for protection on their helmets (without crests) and their round shields which were about 90 cm in diameter (figure 58).

The bulk of the republican legion consisted of more heavily armed infantry known as *hastati, principes* and *triarii*. Each man carried a slightly convex, oval shield about 75 cm wide and 1.20 m tall. This was made of two layers of wood glued together and covered with a layer of canvas and then a layer of calf-skin. The edges were protected by iron bindings and there was an iron boss at the centre. Sculptural evidence also seems to show a reinforcing rib running from top to bottom. The soldiers wore bronze greaves, tied behind the knee, calf and ankle, and a helmet. This carried a crest of three feathers which were dyed black or purple and stood upright to a height of 45 cm. The wealthier men wore a coat of chain mail but the standard form of body armour was a brass chest-protector about 22 cm square. This may have been worn over leather armour (figures 59 and 60).

Each man carried a sword (*gladius*) which was about 60 cm long and hung on the right side of the body. The *triarii*, veterans who formed the rear line in battle, carried long thrusting spears (*hastae*; figure 59). The *principes* and *hastati*, however, were equipped with a special kind of throwing spear called a *pilum* (figure 60). This was made of a thick wooden shaft about 1.35 m long and a barbed iron head of the same length. The head was sunk into the shaft for about half of its length and rivetted firmly into place. The *pilum* was heavy enough to penetrate most armour but, if an enemy soldier caught it in his shield, the weight of the wooden shaft bent the iron head so that the shaft hung down, making the shield virtually useless. Since *pila* were thrown just before the opposing armies met in hand-to-hand fighting their effect could be devastating.

58   A *veles* of the early second century BC

59   A *triarius* of the early second
century BC

60   A *hastatus* of the early second
century BC

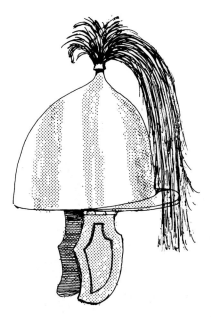

By the middle of the first century BC these different types of soldier had been replaced by a legionary with standardized equipment. Traditionally this change was the work of the Roman general Marius in the years around 100 BC but it seems more likely that the change took place gradually. The legionary of this period wore mail armour similar to that worn earlier but greaves were now apparently only worn by officers. Helmets were again similar to the earlier ones but some sculptures show the crests in several different forms suggesting that they were by this time made of horsehair (figure 61). Each legionary carried two *pila*, a sword and a convex oval shield.

The Early Empire – The Legions

Following the civil wars of the first century BC the emperor Augustus thoroughly reformed the empire's armed forces, creating a standing army of almost 300,000 men. The legionary of the first century AD could be equipped with a variety of armour. An assortment of helmet types are known, made of bronze or iron. All of them, however, had a neck-guard at the rear, cheek-pieces and a peak rivetted above the rim. Crests were now worn only for ceremonial occasions (figure 62).

61 The legionary helmet of the first century BC

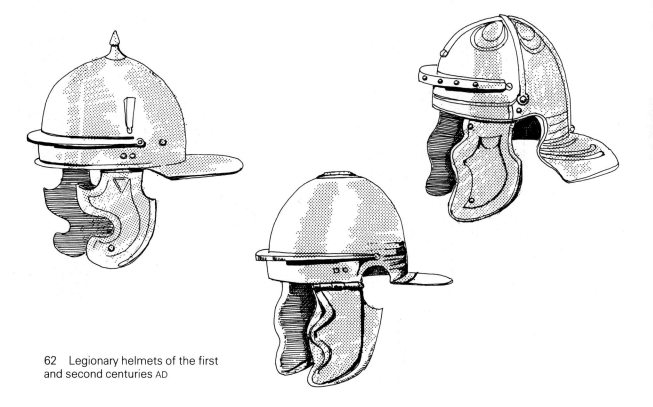

62 Legionary helmets of the first and second centuries AD

Many legionaries wore a new form of armour, introduced late in the first century BC and known by the modern name of the *lorica segmentata* (figure 63). This is the armour traditionally associated with the Roman legions. The *lorica segmentata* was made up of steel strips secured inside by leather straps and closed over the body by buckles, pins and leather thongs. It was easier and cheaper to make than mail and, while it seems that the fittings were liable to break, they were also easy to repair. It should also be noted that scenes on Trajan's Column in Rome show legionaries doing strenuous manual work while wearing their armour, so it clearly did not impede movement too severely. A scarf was worn at the neck to prevent the edges of the strips chafing the skin. Throughout the first and second centuries AD the *lorica segmentata* grew simpler, with the strips becoming broader and fewer in number.

Despite the popular association of this kind of armour with the legionary, it is clear from pieces of sculpture that many legionaries (especially in the eastern provinces) wore mail or scale armour. Mail followed the pattern set earlier. Scale armour was made up of a large number of small bronze or iron plates. These were pierced and fastened together in overlapping rows, rather like the tiles on a roof (figure 64). The completed assemblage of scales was then fixed to a backing, probably of coarse linen. In an excavated example straw padding had been placed between the linen and the scales.

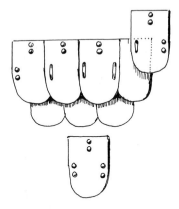

64   Scale armour

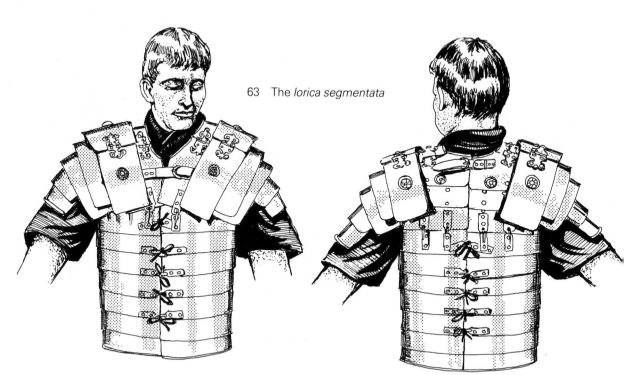

63   The *lorica segmentata*

The legionary's shield was now a semi-cylinder, formed by removing the top and bottom of the old oval form. It was made of plywood, (figure 65), with three layers of wood glued at right angles to each other and covered with leather. The edges were bound with iron or bronze strips. A central hole was crossed by a strut which formed the handgrip. This hole was covered at the front by a metal boss with a broad plate that was rivetted to the shield. The front of the shield was decorated with applied bronze fittings in the shape of thunderbolts.

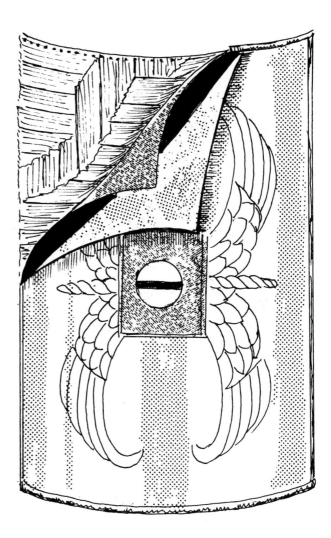

65   The legionary shield

Beneath his armour the legionary (figure 66) wore a simple woollen tunic which had short sleeves and reached to the knees. Normally he went bare-legged but if the climate required it he could wear tight-fitting trousers which came to just below the knees. In addition he might wear the heavy military cloak, the *sagum*, described in chapter three. On his feet he wore *caligae*. These were strong leather sandals, their soles made up of several thicknesses of leather and studded with iron hobnails. Thongs ran from the sandals half way up the shin. In bad weather they could be stuffed with wool or fur for added protection.

He still carried two *pila* and a sword. The sword was now slung from a baldric going over the left shoulder, while a dagger hung from the belt. Also suspended from the belt was a kind of apron of metal-studded leather straps. Opinion is divided on whether this was intended to protect the stomach and genitals or was essentially decorative. Certainly it became much shorter as time went on. The *pilum* was basically similar to those already described but now had a small, pyramidal head which increased its power of penetration and, in the first century AD, it was made heavier by the addition of a spherical lead weight to the shaft.

66 A legionary of the first century AD

As in most armies the officers and NCOs wore distinctive uniforms. Senior officers wore expensive versions of mail armour or a bronze 'muscle cuirass' (figure 67). This was based on a Greek original and was made of metal back and breast plates which were shaped like a naked male torso. Rows of leather straps called *pteruges* hung below the shoulders and waist of the muscle cuirass. It continued in use as late as the fifth century AD, showing the strength of Greek traditions among the Romans. Officers also wore a better quality cloak known as a *paludamentum* (see chapter three).

67   An officer of the first century AD

The centurions, the junior officers and NCOs of the Roman army, wore greaves, mail or scale body armour and helmets (figure 68). Their helmets were essentially the same as those of the average legionary but they had a distinctive crest that ran from side to side rather than from back to front. Standard bearers and musicians also wore mail or scale body armour (figure 69). In addition they wore animal skins over their helmets. The upper part of the animal's head fitted over the helmet and the forepaws were then knotted on the chest to hold it in position.

68   A centurion of the first century AD in scale armour

69   A standard-bearer (*signifer*) and a musician (*cornicen*)

The Early Empire – The Auxiliaries

The auxiliaries present a very varied picture as they included specialist cavalry and infantry units recruited from a variety of peoples and were, at least originally, often equipped in their native fashion. The Roman historian Arrian, writing early in the second century AD, describes armoured and unarmoured cavalry, sometimes riding horses protected with armour themselves. These cavalrymen could be armed with bows, with javelins or with long lances, and they might or might not carry shields. A similar range of equipment existed among the infantry.

In general, however, there was a tendency over the years towards the use of more standardized equipment. Many auxiliaries, both cavalry and infantry, would have worn mail or scale armour over a tunic and trousers similar to those already described (figure 70). They also seem generally to have used the old style oval shields made from plywood in the same way as the legionary's semi-cylindrical one. Their helmets were initially simpler versions of the legionary type but cavalry helmets tended to become deeper and more enclosing as time went on.

70 An auxiliary infantryman of the second century AD

45

The Later Empire

By the fourth century AD the Roman army had changed considerably. The cavalry had replaced the legions as the elite force and there was now little real difference between the various units of infantry. The *lorica segmentata* seems to have gone out of use early in the third century and the late Roman infantryman wore mail or scale armour, or even apparently no armour at all in some units (figure 71). The infantry had (in common with the cavalry) adopted long trousers and long-sleeved tunics. The trousers were worn tucked into boots which replaced the earlier sandals. Shields were now larger and oval or circular in shape. A long sword had been adopted from the cavalry in place of the short *gladius*. Although some units continued to use weighted missiles descended from the *pilum*, most infantry now carried a long thrusting spear.

The cavalry was still made up of men armed in a variety of ways. A new form of armour had been adopted in the third century AD and was worn by some troops. This was lamellar armour, made up of long, thin plates or *lamellae*. These were laced together horizontally and vertically in such a manner that they overlapped each other from the bottom up rather than from the top down as was the case with the scales in scale armour (figure 72). The *lamellae* were made either from metal or from laquered rawhide, which was almost as strong as metal and had the advantage of being considerably lighter. Lamellar armour seems to have been favoured by some officers of the period as well.

71   An infantryman of the fourth century AD

72   Lamellar armour

46

One particular type of late Roman cavalryman, known as a *clibanarius*, was particularly heavily armoured, with special protection for thighs and arms as well as for the torso (figure 73). This type of heavily defended cavalryman was copied from the Persian army after Roman experiences of fighting against them.

The late form of the helmet was also copied from the east. It consisted of a hemispherical bowl, made in two parts and joined by a ridge running from front to back. Attached to this were cheek-pieces, a small neck-protector and, in the case of the cavalry, a nose-guard. The infantry helmet was similar but lacked the nose-guard (figures 71 and 73).

73 A *clibanarius* of the fourth century AD

7 Roman Britain

As we saw in chapter one the Roman empire was a patchwork of many different peoples, each with its own traditions. Although 'Roman' costume would have been found throughout the empire, in the provinces many would still have worn their native dress, particularly during the earlier years of the Roman occupation of the region.

We have already seen how garments such as the Gallic *caracalla* and the Dalmatian *dalmatica* came to be included among 'Roman' clothes and how Greek dress exerted a sustained influence on the Romans from the time of the republic onwards.

In the eastern provinces in particular a number of exotic forms of dress continued to be worn which owed nothing to Roman (or even Greek) traditions. Typical of these are the aristocratic couple shown here (figure 74) from the city of Edessa in Syria.

Roman Britain

Britain was twice visited by Julius Caesar in 55 and 54 BC, but it was not until AD 43 that the emperor Claudius actually began the conquest of the island. By the 80's the Romans controlled all of Britain south of the later line of Hadrian's Wall, although the frontier did not finally settle on this line for several decades thereafter. Everything south of that line remained a province of the empire until the early years of the fifth century AD.

The historian Tacitus tells us that it was official policy to encourage the British leaders to adopt Roman ways. He maintains that under the guidance of his father-in-law Agricola (governor of Britain, 78-84) the Britons so eagerly adopted the *toga* that it was seen everywhere.

The surviving representations of the Romano-Britons – found primarily on their stone funerary monuments – seem to suggest that Roman dress did become common here, although there are no certain cases of the *toga* being worn. Certainly all of the funerary monuments show the deceased dressed in what is essentially Roman style.

Tunics

Both men and women wore tunics with sleeves varying in length from above the elbows to the wrists. Male tunics varied in length but could reach to well below the knees (figures 75 and 76). A smith, whose

74

75

76

74 Man and woman from Edessa,
Syria

75 Man in a tunic and *paenula*

76 Man in a long tunic and cloak

monument survives at York, wore the shorter, off-the-shoulder *exomis* (figure 77).

Women's tunics were regularly ankle-length. Children in the Roman period were dressed as miniature versions of their parents (figures 24 and 35; colour plate 4) and the monument of Vacia, a three year old girl (figure 78), shows her dressed in a long under-tunic with elbow-length sleeves. Above this she wears a sleeveless over-tunic kept in place by a plaited belt. Around her neck is a piece of material which either represents a hooded *alicula* of very truncated form or the upper part of her over-tunic which has a fold of the material turned down at the neck and has then been pinned along her shoulders.

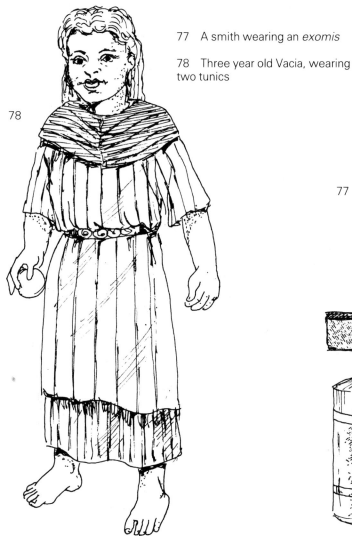

78

77   A smith wearing an *exomis*

78   Three year old Vacia, wearing two tunics

77

Mature women wore the *stola* or, later, the *colobium* or *dalmatica* (figure 79), often over a long *tunica interior* which sometimes shows at the feet (figure 80) or the wrists (figure 81).

79

80

81

79   Julia Brica in a *dalmatica* and *palla*

80   A woman wearing a fringed wrap and holding a fan

81   Regina in a *tunica interior* below a *dalmatica*

Wraps

A number of shawls or wraps are shown on the monuments. The tombstone of Victor (figure 82) shows him reclining on a couch wearing a *pallium* over his tunic, while Julia Brica (figure 79) wears a *palla*. Rather more like the modern shawl is the fringed wrap shown on figure 80. The tombstone of a woman which has been found at Chester (figure 83) shows her wearing a scarf-like shawl with long, straight fringed ends.

Cloaks

In a climate such as Britain's, protection against bad weather would have been particularly necessary and it comes as no surprise that cloaks occur quite frequently on the monuments. We have already seen what may be an *alicula* (figure 78) while a man from London wears a *paenula* (figure 75). A man on a tombstone from Housesteads on Hadrian's Wall wears a fringed cloak pinned at the right shoulder (figure 84), probably a *sagum*. In the emperor Diocletian's price edict the *birrus britannicus* is mentioned as one of the better qualities of *birri* so it is clear that this hooded cloak was also worn in Britain (see figure 26).

An entire family wearing cloaks is shown on a tombstone found at York (figure 85). The stone was erected by Gaius Aeresius, a former soldier with the Sixth Legion, to his wife Flavia Augustina, who died at 39, and their children, who both died before they were two. Each member of the family is shown wearing a long tunic with a cloak over it. The parents and their son each have a *paenula* with a hood, although the hood is not raised. Their little daughter seems to have a wrap or cloak draped over her shoulders and hanging loose.

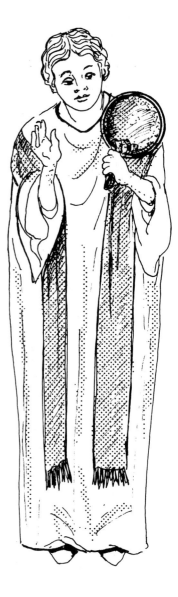

83   Woman wearing a shawl and carrying a mirror

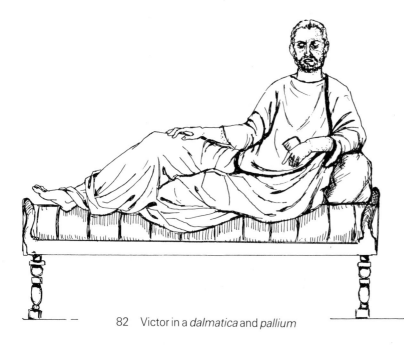

82   Victor in a *dalmatica* and *pallium*

84 Man in a tunic and a probable *sagum*

85 Gaius Aeresius and his family in tunics and cloaks. Gaius holds a scroll, his wife a purse, the children balls

Although the evidence of the monuments seems conclusive we can, however, legitimately doubt how complete a picture they give us of the costume worn in Roman Britain. The majority of them come from the towns of southern Britain and the military districts of the north – exactly those sites where the impact of Roman culture was strongest. Indeed the erection of such Roman monuments argues for a high degree of Romanization and this is likely to be reflected in the style of dress shown.

In some cases we can show that the evidence is incomplete. We have no surviving representations of socks being worn yet a letter written on a wooden tablet recently excavated at Vindolanda near Hadrian's Wall mentions, among other things, woollen socks being sent to the recipient of the letter. Examples of socks themselves have been found in Roman graves in northern Gaul.

The bulk of the population of Roman Britain would have continued to live in the countryside and work the land, living a life relatively unaffected by Romanization. The archaeological evidence suggests that weaving was commonly carried out on these rural sites so we should probably picture most of these country dwellers dressed in homespun woollens of varying quality.

86   Man dressed in Celtic style

In these circumstances it is likely that pre-Roman, Celtic styles of dress continued to be commonly worn. We have no British Celtic representations of themselves but their cousins on the continent have left us some and we can flesh out the picture from the works of Greek and Roman artists and writers. From these sources we know that Celtic men wore ankle-length trousers with belted tunics (figure 86) and, where necessary, cloaks (the *sagum* was in origin Celtic). Women wore long tunics (figure 87) with similar cloaks. Ancient writers comment on the Celtic love of bright colours and on their habit of wearing clothes with striped, checked or multicoloured woven patterns (colour plate 8).

87   Woman dressed in Celtic style

8 Accessories

In this final chapter we will look at certain aspects of dress such as hairstyles, footwear and cosmetics. While not all of these deal strictly with items of clothing, they do, however, help us to form a more detailed picture of the appearance of the Romans.

88 Male hairstyle of the end of the first century BC

Hair

Under the early republic men seem to have worn their hair long and to have had beards. Later tradition maintained that Publius Titinius Mena brought the first barber to Rome from Sicily in 300 BC. Certainly by the later republic and in the early empire it was customary for men to have short hair simply combed and to be clean-shaven (figure 88). The emperor Hadrian, however, set a new fashion by growing a beard and having his hair curled (figure 89). Since Roman barbers were equipped with shears, not scissors, and seem to have used only water on the face prior to shaving it one can understand Hadrian's desire to minimize their attentions.

During the third century AD the succession of short-lived military emperors wore both hair and beard closely cropped. With the emperor Constantine in the early fourth century shaving once again came back into fashion.

Female hair styles present a much more complicated picture. In the time of Augustus the poet Ovid said that women had as many ways of dressing their hair as there were bees in Hybla (a town famous for its honey). Generally though, the styles used in the late republic and at the start of the first century AD were fairly simple, with plaits, buns and waves all in evidence (figure 90). Pins and ribbons were used to hold the hair in place.

By the later first century AD much more elaborate styles had come into favour among women of the upper classes, with a high crest of curls in front and the hair plaited behind (figure 91). Roman satirists wrote of the hours of trouble it took to achieve such styles and it seems likely that in many cases false hair-pieces were used to create the more dramatic effects. Wigs and hair-pieces were certainly worn by both sexes and hair was even imported into the empire for this purpose. From the later second century there was a reaction against such elaborate coiffures and women's hairstyles thereafter reverted to simpler types based on waves and plaits.

89 Male hairstyle of the second century AD

90 Female hairstyle of the mid-first century BC

Cosmetics

Fashionable Romans, sometimes of both sexes, might use make-up. The skin was whitened with chalk or white lead and the cheeks and lips rouged with paints derived from various sources. Ashes or antimony were used to blacken the eyebrows and around the eyes. Blemishes of the skin were covered with *splenia*, small circles or shapes of cloth which were stuck on.

In addition to this the hair might be dyed black or given a golden tinge by using a wash known as *sapo*. Pliny the Elder describes this as being made of a mixture of goat's fat and beech ash.

Jewellery

The wearing of jewellery was largely restricted to Roman women. Rings were the only items commonly worn by men, although both sexes used brooches to fasten clothes. The satirists claimed that men might wear up to sixteen rings. It was a peculiarity of the Romans that they wore rings on any joint of the finger.

Women wore tiaras (figure 32), earrings of various sorts (figures 45 and 99), bracelets and anklets (figure 42) and necklaces (figure 45). In each case these ranged from simple items of bronze and glass-paste or enamel to elaborate creations in gold with jewels inset into them.

One particular item of jewellery is worth a special note. This is the *bulla*, an ornament worn by children to safeguard them from misfortune. Among the poor the *bulla* might be as simple as a knotted leather cord around the neck but children from wealthy families wore a chain suspending a hollow golden globe (figure 24). Inside this was a protective amulet.

91 Female hairstyle of the late first century AD

Footwear

The Romans were highly skilled leatherworkers and most of their shoes were made solely from leather, usually from the hides of cattle.

The simplest form of shoe was the *carbatina*, a single piece of tanned or untanned leather which was secured around the foot by thongs (figure 92). However, most Roman shoes were made up of a single piece upper, usually sewn at the back, fixed to a greater or lesser number of layers forming the sole. The layers of the sole were fixed together either by hobnails or by rawhide thongs. The uppers were fixed along their lower edge between the two top layers of the sole (figure 93). Sandals were made in the same way, with the ends of the straps fixed between the layers of sole.

The Romans divided their footwear into three types – closed boots (*calcei*), sandals (*soleae*) and *crepidae*, which were mid-way between the two. *Calcei* were fastened by thongs which closed the boot and wound around the ankle and lower leg (figure 22). It was a privilege of senators to wear red *calcei*. A taller form of boot which was pulled on to the foot was called a *cothurnus* (figure 20). A *pero* was similar to a *calceus* but was made from untanned leather and was worn in the country during bad weather.

Crepidae (figure 94) generally had much reduced uppers which allowed a large part of the foot to show. The upper was formed either of a low rim with large loops (*ansae*) through which laces ran or of a skeleton of openwork straps which were similarly laced. One type of *crepida* was the military boot, the *caliga* (figure 66).

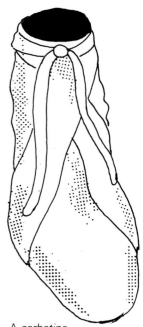

92   A *carbatina*

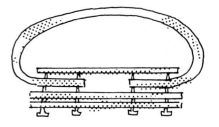

93   Cross-section through a Roman shoe showing construction

94   A *crepida*

Sandals (*solea*) were generally fitted to the foot by a strap or straps across the instep joined to a thong between the big and second toes (figure 31). While *calcei* and *crepidae* were worn out of doors, sandals were regarded as indoor wear, as were *socci* (loose slippers; figure 95). Identical in form to the *solea* was the *baxea*, a cheap sandal made of plaited vegetable fibres like willow or palm leaves.

Two other items of footwear existed which were not made of leather. The *udo* was a warm, close-fitting felt boot used in cold weather while the *sculponea* was a wooden shoe worn for agricultural work. It is unclear whether *sculponeae* were all wood, like Dutch clogs, or had wooden soles with leather uppers. The latter seems more likely and examples of such a shoe have been found (colour plate 3).

Leather shoes could be decorated in a number of ways. The leather might be coloured, like the senator's red *calcei*, or stamped with raised designs. Alternatively it might be cut away, either with a knife or with punches, to produce incredibly elaborate openwork designs (figure 96).

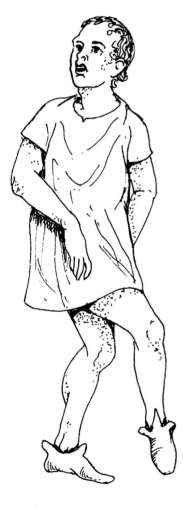

95   A child wearing *socci*

96   An elaborately decorated leather shoe

Hats

Hats were not commonly worn by the Romans. Generally their place was taken by a fold of the *toga* (colour plate 4) or *palla* (figure 34) or by a hood attached to a cloak (figure 26). However certain types of headgear were known. The hood (*cucullus*) was sometimes worn as a separate garment in its own right (figure 97), with long lappets hanging down which could be used to tie it in place. Two hats were adopted from the Greeks and tended to be used by the lower classes although the upper classes also wore them while travelling or in bad weather. These were the *petasus*, a broad-brimmed hat (figure 98), and the *pilleolum*, a conical cap (colour plate 3). The word *pilleus*, often used to describe the *pilleolum*, seems in fact to have been a generic word for 'hat'. Both the *pilleolum* and the *petasus* were commonly made of felt.

Women also wore a variety of headdresses and veils (figures 45 , 48 and 50) together with hairnets made of plaited thread (figures 99 and 40). In addition, a ribbon (*vitta*) was commonly bound around the head to keep the hair in place. Our evidence suggests that an unmarried girl wore a single band while a matron's was double. *Vittae* could be of any colour and were sometimes ornately decorated or studded with pearls.

98   A *petasus*

97   A man wearing a *cucullus*

Miscellaneous accessories

The Romans, like ourselves, frequently carried around with them a variety of items of practical use. Money was carried either in a *marsupium*, a leather pouch closed by a draw-string (figure 85), or was stowed inside the folds of the girdle fastening the tunic. Bulkier objects were carried in a *crumena*, a kind of satchel usually slung from the neck (colour plate 3).

From late republican times it was common to carry around a *sudarium*, a linen cloth which was used to wipe the face. If someone had no *sudarium* then they would use a corner of their clothing. By the later third century AD the *sudarium* was known as an *orarium* or *mucinium* and was certainly used like the modern handkerchief. It is not clear whether this was the case earlier or whether noses were then blown using the fingers.

Another linen cloth was the *mappa* or napkin, used at dinner. This was the cloth dropped by the consul to start the chariot races in the circus and is regularly shown as part of the consular regalia (figure 56).

Largely restricted to female use were the *flabellum* and the *umbraculum*. The *flabellum* was a fan made either of feathers or of linen fixed on a frame (figure 80). It was either rigid or collapsable. The *umbraculum* was the equivalent of our parasol and was used only to provide shade not as a protection against rain. It consisted of a light cloth stretched over a wooden framework (figure 100).

Sticks seem to have been carried very rarely (figure 53) and then usually only by the aged or infirm to help them walk. An exception were the sticks carried as symbols of office by, for example, centurions in the army (figure 68).

99   A woman wearing a hair-net

100   An *umbraculum*

Further reading

BOAK, A E R and SINNIGEN, W G, *A History of Rome to AD 565*, London 1965

BONFANTE, L, *Etruscan Dress*, London 1975

CONNOLLY, P, *The Roman Army*, London 1975

GRABAR, A, *Byzantine Painting*, London 1979
A useful source of illustrations for the later period

GRANGER-TAYLOR, H, 'Weaving Clothes to Shape in the Ancient World', *Textile History*, 13 (1982) pp 3-25

HIGGINS, R A, *Greek and Roman Jewellery*, London 1961

HOUSTON, M G, *Ancient Greek, Roman and Byzantine Costume*, London 1947

KENT, J P C, *Roman Coins*, London 1978
Particularly useful as a source of illustrations of hairstyles.

LIVERSIDGE, J, *Britain in the Roman Empire*, London 1968

PALLATTINO, M, *The Etruscans*, London 1974

PICARD, G, *Roman Painting*, London 1970
A useful source of illustrations

STRONG, D and BROWN, D (eds), *Roman Crafts*, London 1976
See especially the contributions by J P Wild on 'Textiles' pp 166-77, and J W Waterer on 'Leatherwork' pp 178-93)

WILSON, L M, *The Clothing of the Ancient Romans*, London 1938

Index